Information Entrepreneurship

Information Services Based on the Information Lifecycle

Susan G. Fowler

The Scarecrow Press, Inc.
Lanham, Maryland • Toronto • Oxford
2005

SCARECROW PRESS, INC.

Published in the United States of America
by Scarecrow Press, Inc.
A wholly owned subsidiary of
The Rowman & Littlefield Publishing Group, Inc.
4501 Forbes Boulevard, Suite 200, Lanham, Maryland 20706
www.scarecrowpress.com

PO Box 317
Oxford
OX2 9RU, UK

British Library Cataloguing in Publication Information Available

Library of Congress Cataloging-in-Publication Data

Fowler, Susan G., 1958–
  Information entrepreneurship : information services based on the information
lifecycle / Susan G. Fowler.
     p. cm.
  Includes bibliographical references and index.
  ISBN 0-8108-5258-6 (pbk. : alk. paper)
  1. Information services. 2. Knowledge management. 3. Organizational learning. 4.
Information storage and retrieval systems. I. Title.

ZA3157.F69 2005
025—dc22

                                                            2004018148

♾™ The paper used in this publication meets the minimum requirements of
American National Standard for Information Sciences—Permanence of
Paper for Printed Library Materials, ANSI/NISO Z39.48-1992.
Manufactured in the United States of America.

*Dedicated to three men in my life:
Roger Greer, who is generous with his
great thoughts; Wayne Fowler, who
gave me the gift of entrepreneurship;
and, Bob Grover, with whom I am
blessed to share my life.*

Contents

Introduction

Upon this gifted age, in its dark hour,
Rains from the sky a meteoric shower
Of facts . . . they lie unquestioned, uncombined.
Wisdom enough to leech us of our ill
Is daily spun; but there exists no loom
To weave it into fabric.
—Edna St. Vincent Millay, "Upon This Age," *Huntsman, What Quarry?*,
1939

When I was introduced to the above Millay quote I was struck at how her words ring true more than sixty years after they were first penned. We have more information available to us than ever before in human history, and yet we're challenged to make sound decisions because, too frequently, the glut of information is overwhelming.

Millay's "loom to weave it into fabric" is the domain of the information profession. Regardless of the tools we use—research, information systems development, knowledge management consulting—we are weaving together a portion of the wisdom that solves business dilemmas, supports decision making and helps create new knowledge.

This book covers what I consider to be the essentials of providing professional information services. It concentrates on the professional service side of business and not the "how-to's" of running a small business. I feel justified in this approach because there are lots of business books out there that will teach you about cash flow and record keeping and all the details that fill a seventy-hour work week. This book is theory-based, which means it does not rely on current technology to ensure success. Theory is considerably more stable than technology, yet once we get the theories down, we can apply them to maximize technology for our clients.

Occasionally my colleagues and I discuss whether client-centeredness is learned or intrinsic. I think it's a combination of internalized values and life experience that causes one to value service to others. In my case, I trace my value of customer service to my childhood. I grew up in the late 1960s and early 1970s in a small, Midwestern town. One of my childhood memories is of the clothing stores that dotted Main Street—in particular, those stores that had seamstresses to make alterations. By providing in-house tailoring service, wearing clothes "off-the-rack" became optional. The alterations provided by the store ensured a customized fit; once you experienced it, off-the-rack felt (literally) a poor second choice. This once common practice has become rare enough to symbolize the best of service and, by extension, higher than average prices. Today, those for whom a tailored fit is important view the slightly higher price as negligible. For those who have never experienced the comfort and convenience of tailoring, the added cost may seem exorbitant.

So it is with information services. Good service, albeit "off-the-rack," can be found in bookstores and libraries. Bookstores and libraries may hire exceptionally talented personnel, but time constraints and workload prevent in-depth service. The customer is on her own and may not realize there is an alternative to doing it herself. Even if the customer is aware of alternatives, unless she has experienced the time and cost savings of working with an information professional, the customer may decide she can save money by doing it herself. The reality is that some people are good "do-it-yourselfers" and some are not. What matters is the motivation behind the "do-it-yourself" approach. Regardless, those who appreciate a high-quality product and are willing to pay for professional-level service make excellent clients.

The "willing to pay for" is a critical characteristic. Everyone wants information; very few are willing to pay for it. The information profession has done an excellent job of providing service and a very poor job of educating its public about the costs involved. The truth is that information services have always cost money, and most public libraries have done an exceptional job of sheltering their clients from that fact. Unless they pay for copies or incur overdue fees, most library patrons do not hand over money during the course of a routine visit. This practice of "something for nothing" leaves many with the erroneous idea that there are no costs associated with running the local public library. And if the library doesn't charge for services, why should anyone else expect to be paid?

The local public library is basic to a democratic society and, in that setting, access to information should be as unencumbered by fees and policies as possible. For those patrons who demand more than basic services, some libraries are offering personalized, in-depth services and charging professional-level fees. This is one way to ensure equitability of scarce professional resources.

Exemplary, customized services may be found in public libraries for added fees. More often they are found among those trained in library science and information management and who work outside of the traditional library setting. Our group is known by a number of names: information brokers, information professionals, freelance librarians and cybrarians. Whatever we call ourselves, we are a diverse group serving an equally diverse clientele with one thing in common: we put our clients first; subsequently, our clients recognize the value of our made-to-order information products. They've done the math and calculated how long it would take their staff to locate and retrieve information and then read, synthesize and repackage it in the format that is most useful to the organization. Locating and/or retrieving information is the easy part; making sense of it and articulating the results in our clients' language is considerably more challenging. It's also how we add value.

Critically reviewing information to ensure accuracy and integrity and providing results in a timely fashion require professional-level skills. When a client contracts for our services, they are not just contracting for a final product. They are also contracting for a professional's "know-how" of retrieval, analysis and customized packaging. It's the "know-how" that separates the professional from the do-it-yourselfer.

Value-added services combine the information professional's expert ability to diagnose the information request, select the best resources to meet the request, analyze the results and, assuming the results are appropriate to the request, package it to meet the client's specific needs. There is a proliferation of information available on the Internet, and much of it is bad, wrong and/or misleading. The information professional knows to check for credentials behind any piece of information; he or she also knows how to judge appropriateness of the information such as reading level or the accuracy of topic.

This book will not resolve the dichotomy between do-it-yourselfers and those who are comfortable contracting for expert information services. However, it is interesting to note that since the Industrial Revolution we have had increasing levels of specification in society. No longer must we raise flax to spin into thread and weave into linen; we go to the fabric shop and buy the yardage. Better yet, we can go shopping—online or in person—and buy ready-made garments. Likewise, we no longer raise all our food. Having grown up on a farm, I am particularly appreciative of being able to purchase eggs and milk at the local grocery store rather than daily collecting those products directly from the source.

Another indication that our society has made routine what (in the United States) was considered luxury is illustrated by the bottled water phenomenon. Despite reports that say bottled water is no safer than American cities' tap water, sales of bottled water continue to roll along. Not too long ago, if a person wanted a drink of water, he or she went in search of a water fountain. Just as public libraries are funded by local and state taxes, so are U.S. city water treatment plants. And, just as most public library patrons do not engage in money exchange, users of a local water fountain can obtain a drink without payment. Today we pay for what used to be free in order to drink it recreationally. We like the convenience of having our hydration source immediately at hand. When traveling, bottled water calms any anxiety we might have regarding the purity of a strange city's tap water. If we can adopt the practice of paying for one publicly provided resource, can we not adopt the practice of paying for what we thought was free (i.e., information) but never was?

Information professionals are known for the value they add to the services they provide. The value that I add to my information services is the customization I provide based on the client's individual learning style, his or her organization's learning style, and other factors that the information needs assessment indicated were of importance. Regardless of the request, each information service begins with such an assessment in order to ensure a true custom fit.

My information business was established over ten years ago, and I am often asked how I got into this line of work. That's what I'm asked; a better question would be how I've stayed in business over the years. Frankly, starting a business is easy. Keeping it going—now, that's the hard part. It's my belief that a business built on client-centered services survives and thrives regardless of the economy.

There are a good number of independent information professionals busily at work in the United States. Most have professional credentials, either earned at a previous "mainstream" job or by academic degree; many belong to professional associations, and, of those, most follow a professional code of ethics. Those who have a code of ethics, whether from a professional association or something they have composed on their own, do so of their own volition. No one can be "disbarred" from the information profession, although a few rogues may get sued and others simply go out of business once word gets out about their business practices. The sad fact is that there is no regulation on my chosen profession, something I sincerely hope will change in my lifetime.

There is plenty of work for talented professionals who are committed to providing excellent customer service. Granted, the official positions may not show up on the company organizational chart, but the opportunities for service certainly exist. It's my hope that this book weaves together a few pieces for readers who are interested in creating a rewarding career of professional information service.

In the final analysis, success in the information business depends on how well we serve our clients. My clients are the most important part of my business, and I hope your clients are the most important part of yours. It is our place as information professionals to view service to clients as an honor, one that we value enough to engage in continual learning and professional growth. Together we can build a loom to weave data into wisdom.

Chapter 1

The Information Profession

Economic downturns can be a good thing for universities. In times of layoffs and employment uncertainty, students flock to finish a bachelor's or start a master's program with the idea that it will make them more marketable. It will if they earn an education instead of just a degree. There is a difference, and it's the former that separates the professionals from the people who merely have extra initials after their names.

Simply put, a professional is an expert, one who possesses a high level of knowledge or skill. The term "profession" indicates a set of required standards in order to hold membership in the profession. Some see the American Library Association (ALA) accredited master's degree in library science as their entry ticket to the information management profession. That might get them in the door, but it's the ability to apply classroom knowledge to real-life information service opportunities that marks the professional. It would be unrealistic to say a new graduate has to perform perfectly. A new graduate with professional promise is able to think and apply the tools he or she acquired during the course of his or her studies. Most importantly, he or she will apply those tools with the client's needs uppermost. Being skilled is of little value if people are not served.

Successful people in our profession tend to be people persons. We recognize that information has no value if it's not used, and it is best used by people. Therefore, we serve people—students, executives, construction workers and musicians—not the packages information arrives in (books, DVDs, newspapers, email). Effective people service is relationship-based. We know the value of building relationships with our clients in order to provide tailored service. Regardless of where we serve—in traditional libraries or cyberspace—we share the goal of providing the client with the right information in the right format. We do this most effectively if we can establish a relationship with our clients, one that allows us to know them well enough to provide high-quality service.

Information is a considerable commodity in today's Western society. Unlike its physical commodity predecessors, information has some unique characteristics that require different rules of management. In his 1985 book, *The Knowledge Executive*, Harlan Cleveland helped us gain a clearer picture of information, namely, that it is a different resource than the physical resources we're more familiar with. Physical resources are finite, can be stored in only one place at a time and have only one owner at a time. Cleveland had several insights about the nature of information, including the five below.

Information is expandable. This refers to information as a whole, which tends to be used and added to and reused. Other commodities cannot be expanded without manufacturing more units, requiring changes in machinery as well as procedures. These alterations come with costs, while information expands through its use and reuse. The highest cost of information is at its creation; duplication involves relatively little cost. What's more, the same information can be expanded simultaneously by different people in different time zones and who speak different languages. Take Einstein's Theory of Relativity ($E = mc^2$). It took the exchange of ideas with other scientists for him to work out this theory prior to its publication in 1915. More importantly, his theory had a profound effect on how we viewed the world in the 20th century. It is a widely accepted theory and continues to be the subject of intense discussion today. Through that discussion, new knowledge is created, and with the dissemination of that knowledge, each of us gets a little wealthier in what we "own" in our personal knowledge banks.

Information is compressible. It wasn't all that long ago that we oohed and aahed over the amount of data we could put on a CD-ROM ("Imagine an entire set of encyclopedias on one disk!"), and now we have PDAs and ZIP disks and USB flash drives with more storage space than the first computers of fifty-some years ago that took up an entire office floor. For that matter, my PDA uses memory cards that are roughly the size of a postage stamp. These memory cards have triple to six times the storage space than the computer I had fifteen years ago. Equally handy are the USB flash drives that can hold critical file backups while swinging conveniently from a neck lanyard or keychain.

Information is transportable. It is also available in a growing number of formats. Print out the document on your 750MB ZIP disk and you have a few thousand pages to tote around. Or, keep the data on the ZIP disk and tote those pages in a conveniently small package weighing a few ounces. Email the files to a colleague and you have transported information while retaining a copy for your own use, without visiting the copy machine and mail room. Another example of transportability is the memory card on my Palm handheld that holds three times what my first hard drive held. I can beam the information from my handheld to another, or I can email it through a wireless connection, such as my cellular telephone. In any case, Cleveland's original point for this characteristic holds true today. If information is transportable, "remoteness is more choice than geography." Technology has made it possible to conduct business from nearly any location on the planet, depending on how much effort one wants to put into it.

Information is diffusive. Cleveland stated with uncanny accuracy, "Information is aggressive, even imperialistic, in striving to break out of the unnatural bonds of secrecy in which thing-minded people try to imprison it." The more it leaks, he went on to say, the more we have and the more of us who have it. Any attempt to keep information on a leash will be successful only for the short term. I always think of the students in Tiananmen Square and the failed attempt in 1991 to reinstate the Soviet Union as examples of this principle. Those oppressive acts were witnessed in real time around the world, despite the wishes of the oppressors. Examples closer to home are the WorldCom and Enron business failures of 2002, with the Enron case being particularly ironic. Not even the shredding of key documents, a flagrant violation of the most basic records management principles, could keep the Enron scandal from breaking.

Information is shareable. I can accommodate several people in my car, but only one of us can drive it. My car is so unique that it is the only car with its vehicle identification number (VIN).

That VIN is stamped on major components of the car, such as the frame, axles and engine. The point is that physical goods can have only one owner at a time. Information is shareable because more than one person can know the same piece of information ($E = mc^2$) at the same time.

The bottom line to Cleveland's description of information is this: it is a powerful resource, one with unique characteristics. Those characteristics prevent us from hoarding, locking away or otherwise suppressing information. We may be able to do that for brief periods of time, but those periods of time are becoming briefer and briefer. In the end, information will seep out and our efforts to suppress it will be found out.

The information economy has characteristics that mandate management techniques profoundly different from those developed to manage physical resources. Likewise, the information economy needs professionals who understand their clients and the information they create, seek, use and re-create. We will discuss information services based on the information lifecycle in subsequent chapters. For now, we'll concentrate on the mindset of the information professional and the general services he or she provides.

Professional Code of Ethics

Attorneys have them; so do physicians. The public may mentally link "malpractice" with a medical case gone awry, but other professionals—including those in information management—can be guilty of committing malpractice.

Malpractice occurs when the profession's code of ethics is breached. The code of ethics serves a dual purpose: to protect the public from unscrupulous frauds and to protect honest professionals from aforementioned charlatans who give our profession a bad name.

Information workers who provide value-added services do so because they wish to save their clients time and money by analyzing and synthesizing information into a useful package customized to the client's needs. This level of service is valuable, but it is time-intensive and therefore can be expensive. Consequently, the temptation often arises to cut corners, which increases the opportunity for malpractice.

Let's say that you have a client who has an idea for a new business and wants to know where it would be most successful, if there are any other businesses like it anywhere, and who its target market would be. Can you locate this information without committing malpractice? Of course you can. Will it increase your business costs? You bet—doing things the right way is rarely inexpensive. Is it worth shaving a few corners just to get the job done and cash the check? No. You might get away with it once, maybe twice. But sloppy work has as long of a shelf-life as high-quality work, and it will come back to haunt you. Your reputation is worth more than the fee from one project.

What constitutes malpractice? Here's a composite definition gleaned from the literature[1]:

- Misrepresentation of oneself to obtain information
- Industrial espionage
- Misrepresentation of the work one can perform
- Presentation of partially completed projects as the final product
- Breach of client or source confidentiality

- Committing an illegal act
- Purposely giving false information
- Incomplete or sloppy research

From this list, you can see what your restrictions would be. First, you have to be truthful as to your identity, but, unless your client has told you otherwise, never reveal your client's name. You can legitimately claim to be someone "doing research" on the topic.

Second, practice legal and appropriate methods of obtaining information on potential business competition. For example, you can glean information from industry or trade publications, review annual reports and conduct interviews. This is an area where more than one professional has been tempted to outsource to less reputable service providers. Unless you do the work yourself or can closely supervise, I recommend against that practice. If you're going to outsource, please do so with another member of our profession who also follows a code of ethics.

Third, if you feel the request is beyond your ability, either refer it to another information professional, subcontract with a partner or turn it down. This may cut into your profits, but better to lose a little now than all clients later.

Lastly, if you decide to take on the project, make sure all the information available is included and that your report is complete. In the scenario of the client establishing a new business, millions of dollars could be involved. For your clients to have legal problems because of your incompetence is a disaster no one needs.

The flip side to this is that by following a code of ethics you deliver top-quality, professional services that enable your client to launch a successful business. Your reward for conducting business ethically is to take satisfaction in a job well done and to enjoy a reputation as an honest professional worthy of repeat business. The stellar reputation is a solid, long-term investment and much more valuable than any short-term rewards.

The Association for Independent Information Professionals (AIIP) has a code of ethics that addresses specific actions by the information professional[2].

An information professional bears the following responsibilities:

- Uphold the profession's reputation for honesty, competence and confidentiality.
- Give clients the most current and accurate information possible within the budget and timeframes provided by the clients.
- Help clients understand the sources of information used and the degree of reliability which can be expected from those sources.
- Accept only those projects which are legal and are not detrimental to our profession.
- Respect client confidentiality.
- Recognize intellectual property rights. Respect licensing agreements and other contracts. Explain to clients what their obligations might be with regard to intellectual property rights and licensing agreements.
- Maintain a professional relationship with libraries and comply with all their rules of access.
- Assume responsibility for employees' compliance with this code.

The AIIP's code of ethics emphasizes the positive things we can and should do. My own professional code of ethics incorporates concepts from the preceding codes. I think it is important to articulate standards of honesty and integrity for my professional behavior. It is a healthy reminder for me and an assurance to my clients that my business sets high standards. As an example:

- I will not misrepresent myself in order to gather information which might otherwise be withheld.
- I will respect the confidentiality of my sources.
- I will respect the rights of information (provide accurate attribution) except when the source requests confidentiality.
- Important matters will be put in writing to ensure a proper understanding of long-term research projects and the retainer relationship with the client.

Whether you adopt AIIP's or another professional organization's code of ethics or write your own, it's important that you do so. Until our profession develops a national standardized certification process similar to what attorneys, accountants and physicians have, our code of ethics is the primary evidence to our clients that demonstrates our professional status.

The remainder of this book focuses on the different services information professionals can provide based on the information lifecycle. In general, we assist with information's creation, use, storage, retrieval, archival and final discard. Proper management at each stage in the lifecycle relies on a solid information infrastructure, which comprises policies, procedures and technology.

The construction industry tells us that the quality of the foundation dictates the strength and integrity of a building. A façade may be very eye-appealing, but it will crumble without the proper support. The same is true for an information system. The best technology in the world will not help a system that has policy and procedural flaws. Information professionals help their clients by ensuring a solid infrastructure from which to grow in today's information-rich environment.

The Information Lifecycle: Its Associated Components and Activities

Information has a lifecycle. It is created, used, stored, retrieved, reused (and possibly re-created), stored again, and so forth until it has outlived its usefulness. Some pieces of information are eternal; most are ephemeral. Regardless, an effective information system is one based on the natural lifecycle. Systems of this design incorporate standard information management requirements with what works for each client organization.

Table 1.1 lists specific professional activities associated with each component of the information lifecycle; figure 1.1 provides a graphical illustration.

Component	Activity
Creation	Assess the infrastructure
Use	Identify communities of practice and identify the organization's information practices
Storage/Retrieval	Develop a retention schedule, establish a standardized system, identify corporate artifacts, establish preservation policies and procedures for all formats (digital, paper, other media)
Archive/Discard	The retention schedule guides associated activities, which may include selection of archival storage materials and/or locating bonded shredding services that guarantee confidentiality

Table 1.1   Client Needs Assessment Guidelines

It is important to recognize that the activities and components associated with each stage of the information lifecycle are dynamic. They influence each other in a symbiotic arrangement. The underlying infrastructure affects every stage of the lifecycle, but corporate practices influence whether information is created and used. A corporate structure that values organizational learning needs an information system that supports heavy use; a corporate structure that discourages information sharing needs a different type of infrastructure. The example in this book assumes a corporate client that values heavy use of information. However, corporations on both ends of the spectrum—and all types in between—need information systems. It is not a question of whether to design an effective information system, but when.

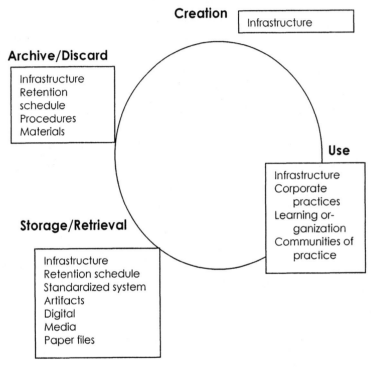

Creation

Infrastructure

Archive/Discard

Infrastructure
Retention
schedule
Procedures
Materials

Use

Infrastructure
Corporate
    practices
Learning or-
    ganization
Communities of
    practice

Storage/Retrieval

Infrastructure
Retention schedule
Standardized system
Artifacts
Digital
Media
Paper files

Figure 1.1   The Information Lifecycle

The next chapter focuses on the most important skill an information professional can have: accurately diagnosing information needs by understanding how one's client thinks and processes information.

Notes

1. Mintz, *Library Journal*, September 14, 1985.
2. www.aiip.org/.

Chapter 2

A People-First Philosophy

Knowledge requires a knower. [1]
—Patrick Wilson

Information has no value if people cannot access and use it. This chapter addresses the importance of understanding one's clients in order to design and deliver an information package customized to the client's needs.

The preceding chapter addressed why client-centered services are intrinsic to the information professional's approach. In a world of "Wal-Mart" mentality (cheapest is best), we have to provide that something extra that places our services above what anyone could or would do themselves. That something extra is customization, and to customize, we need to know our customers.

Customization gives us an edge over the "do it yourself" attitude. Since few actually deliver on their promise for high-quality service, that gives us another edge over the competition. Besides, it's the right thing to do. Our profession has historically tried to do the right thing by our clients. During the dark ages of librarianship, we jealously hoarded books and materials from the public and justified our actions as the most efficient means of preserving those materials for future generations. While we can dispense with the information hoarding, we must retain our focus on the client.

Mass-produced information shifted our emphasis from protecting a few resources to filtering out the best slice for a particular client in a particular circumstance. This has had significant influence in transforming our profession's attitude from "protect and restrict" to "unfettered access for all." Access is one thing; retrieval, use and comprehension are other challenges. That is where information professionals come in. We provide access and teach information skills to our clients' organizations. We read, synthesize and customize the final product. In short, our services go a long way toward building Millay's loom that solves our client's problems. We do this best if we have a "people-first" mindset.

What do we mean by people first? It means we value people highly enough to tailor our professional skills in a manner that will benefit them the most. It means we take time to get to know our clients and the situation in which the information will be used. We don't expect them to learn our profession; we use the tools and skills of our profession to serve them. As way of illustration, imagine a dentist who expects the patient to pinpoint his microscopic cavity or the attorney who expects her client to be fully versed in appropriate legal precedents. Professionals like the dentist and attorney provide service based on professional expertise, and information professionals are no different. Like our medical and legal professional colleagues, we use the tool of diagnosis.

Diagnosis

Professionals must be able to diagnose a problem, prescribe or recommend a solution, implement the solution and evaluate the results. A study by Grover and Carabell (1995) of health professionals showed similarities in the diagnostic process despite the diversity of professionals interviewed. These similarities were extended to diagnosis practiced by the information profession, typically found in the "reference interview." Traditionally we have used diagnosis in regard to information searches, and that is how we will start the discussion here. However, diagnosis is an effective tool for any information problem, whether it's to search and retrieve or to design and build an information infrastructure.

An Overview of Diagnosis

1. Diagnosis is a systematic process used for examining problems.
2. The foundation for diagnosis is a knowledge base.
3. Diagnosis is determined on an individual basis.
4. Proper diagnosis views problems from the client's perspective.
5. Diagnoses must be continually evaluated.
6. Diagnosis is holistic, combining theory, skill, and intuition.
7. Diagnosis, because of its complexity, is an art.

—Grover and Carabell, 1995

Figure 2.1   Diagnosis Overview

Like other professions' use of diagnosis, the information diagnostic experience is recursive and based on the information user's unique qualities, including context, environment, culture, cognitive style and expected use of the information. As Carol Kuhlthau noted, the diagnostic exchange is shaped as much by the user's learning during the information seeking process as it is the original question. What may be "relevant at the beginning of a search may later turn out to be irrelevant, and vice versa" (1993, p. 3). The key is to have the client and the information professional engaged in a conversation during the information seeking period to establish how on-target the results are to the information need.

Diagnosis begins with a data-gathering interview. The professional wants to find out how the problem began, how the client perceives the problem, how the problem impacts the client's life, and what type of solution the client wants. It is important to develop rapport with the client, and some professionals may find it difficult to keep an open mind, much less avoid the tendency to predict answers and outcomes. Information professionals in particular are very, very good at retrieving information, and it is easy to get lulled into believing that "all" the client needs is the proper information delivered. Take the time to gather all the data for a full diagnosis, even if you think you know your client or have worked with him or her in the past. People and circumstances change, so what might have worked in the past may not be effective this time. Again, it is the difference between tailor-made and off-the-rack, with the former requiring diagnosis for the customized fit.

Although Grover and Carabell point out that there is no single, definitive way of conducting a diagnostic interview, they do offer a general framework for a successful diagnosis:

1. Establish a comfortable client-professional relationship
2. Determine the context for the information need
3. Determine the information use preferences of the user
4. Ascertain limitations the user may have
5. Continuously evaluate the effectiveness of the diagnosis in identifying and addressing the information needs of the client.

This list reminds us of what we discussed in earlier chapters. An information professional needs to be a people-person in order to establish rapport and empathize with the client's information need situation. People skills are needed to conduct the interviews related to a diagnosis, both in the ability to phrase the questions best suited to the client and in the ability to listen carefully to the client's verbal and non-verbal responses.

As we discussed in earlier chapters, anyone can solve an information problem without hiring an information professional. When we say we provide "service," what are we saying? We're saying that we have a body of knowledge that allows us to:

- Do it faster
- Get exactly what is needed
- Sift out and deliver only what the client can use
- Repackage the information to supply the best quality available in the client's information processing level

Diagnosis in a Related Profession: Database Development

In order to provide professional service, we start with the diagnostic process, during which we identify what the client wants and, more importantly, what the client needs. Balancing the two requires professional judgment. In later chapters we will discuss the design and implementation of an information infrastructure that supports the lifecycle of information. With that in mind, and a desire to demonstrate the commonality of diagnosis across professions, I asked John Holland of Propaganda3 in Kansas City, Missouri, to describe the use of diagnosis in his work as a database developer. His answers underscore the similarity between professions. Because we share professional values such as diagnosis, we enjoy a collaborative relationship.

SGF: Do you use a systematic process for examining problems?
JH: Short answer, yes.
      Long answer, yes. The first thing I have to do is to get an understanding of the overall system where the problem is occurring. I meet with the client and have them describe what they see the problem as, then I ask questions to make sure there are no communication problems, and we are talking about the same things. This provides a solid base of understanding to apply to all decisions made moving forward.
SGF: How much of your process is derived from formal education, and how much is derived from experience?
JH: I would say the majority of how I diagnose problems is derived from experience. Formal education provided a base when I began doing what I do now, but over time, experience has become more important.
SGF: Do you use the same diagnostic process for each client?

JH: Yes and no. The manner in which I design a database is the same, but each client is different and each has their own way of communicating things, so I have to ask the questions differently to get the information I am looking for.

SGF: Would you agree that "proper diagnosis views problems from the client's perspective"?

JH: Most certainly. The key, I believe, is to be able to view the problem from the client's perspective, yet be able to tap into my experience from resolving past problems to solve this particularly unique problem.

SGF: Please describe how the iterative process of database design corresponds with the statement, "diagnoses must be continually evaluated."

JH: A database design must provide for flexibility. The database is usually the part of an application that I would want to change the least. Therefore, I take great pains to build structures, constraints and triggers that will support the data structures correctly even when the application itself is reevaluated and changed.

SGF: You've already said that database design is largely intuitive. Is the above statement correct in saying that diagnosis, in your case the database design process—is an art?

JH: Yes. Database design, to me, is like designing the foundation of a house. If I was going to build a house that sits on a foundation, I wouldn't build the house then think about building the foundation. The same is true for building applications that are data-based. There is no way to foresee every obstacle, but you can limit the number that you have to deal with by giving the design of the database great thought and attention before anything is built.

More often than not, people want to start thinking about application flow before they have given any thought to what is going to support those applications. I think the complete opposite way, I always think about the database and how it will support what the client wants to do. That usually gives us the opportunity to resolve issues that would not have come up until much later during the build phase.

SGF: Are there other points you'd like to make?

JH: I said before database design is an art. I was wrong. GOOD database design is an art, bad database design is horrific. I have seen good design and bad.

Good database design makes it easy to interface with an application and makes allowances for expansion and growth with little change in structure. With bad database design, I would find myself continuously trying to find workarounds to combat structures that are storing severely redundant data or a database with no data integrity so child records would be orphaned and hence cluttering up the data.

And so it is for information professionals and the solutions we build for our clients. Let's keep in mind John's ending comments: Good design is an art; bad design is horrific. May we always practice the art of information science and keep our clients' unique needs in mind as we design solutions to their problems.

Services for the Individual: The Who, How and What

Customized services for an individual begin by understanding three things about our client—the *who*, the *how* and the *what*. *Who* refers to "Who is this person as an individual?" and *how* refers to "How does this person process information?" The *what* we'll address shortly. Finding the answers to these questions is important because individuals are very different, and we cannot customize our services unless we understand those individual differences. These questions are usually answered through a brief interview that may be conducted in person, over the phone or by email—whichever means is most convenient for the client.

For in-person interviews, I focus on identifying the information need and the urgency of the need. I can usually accomplish this through a few brief questions, such as, "Tell me what you already know about [the subject]," "Help me understand how you plan to use the information," and, based on the answers to those questions, "So [format X] would be your first preference for the results? How soon do you need this?" I also try to make it clear that follow-up questions on my part may be expected and are a natural part of the information seeking process.

A brief aside on these "quick and dirty" reference situations—a tip I picked up from a fellow professional years ago has served me well for new clients. I tell them I'll do a free, fifteen-minute scan to see what is available and get back to them. That way they know what's feasible and I can give them a more accurate estimate of my fee.

For more complex information services, such as designing information infrastructures that include records management and archival systems, I prefer to go more in-depth in my analysis of the client organization. Whereas I might be able to get a "feel" for an individual's learning style preferences in a single reference request, I prefer to be more systematic when I'm dealing with several individuals or a formal organization. In these situations, I use several instruments, one of which I base on a framework derived from both the Myers-Briggs Type Indicator (MBTI) and Howard Gardner's theory of multiple intelligences. I ask questions based on MBTI and multiple intelligences not as a "scientific" survey but as a means to give me a general idea of the individual's learning and processing preferences. It's not unusual to find relative homogeneity within smaller work units of an overall heterogeneous organization. This gives me a micro view of a work unit and the ability to frame that within the macro view of the overall organization.

It's important to keep in mind that learning styles are preferences, which means they're not etched in stone and that they can change based on environment and situation. Also, "different" is OK and even welcome in organizations. Heterogeneity may be a challenge to manage, but the strength of diverse ideas and opinions is well worth the effort.

Sample questions from the instrument I use are in the resources section at the end of this book. But first, let's look at some background on the MBTI and Gardner's multiple intelligences.

MBTI and Multiple Intelligences

The MBTI is based on Carl Jung's psychological types (1971). The mother and daughter team of Katherine Myers and Isabel Briggs (1962) developed the Type Indicator as a way to apply Jung's types. The MBTI demonstrates how people prefer to gather, process and use information. The preferences are:

Intake of information	Introvert (I) or Extravert (E)
Data gathering	Sensing (S) or Intuitive (N)
Decision making	Thinking (T) or Feeling (F)
Lifestyle	Judging (J) or Perceiving (P)

Table 2.1   MBTI Types

The MBTI is not a personality test but a measure of how an individual prefers to handle information. Therefore, it is possible to have an introvert type who is quite sociable and an extravert who is quite shy. There are sixteen possible types under the Myers-Briggs Type Indicator, and, as might be expected, some types are more complementary than others. When types are not complementary, the ensuing tension is often interpreted as a personality conflict, when in reality it is only a difference in learning style preferences. A better understanding of each type can help clear up this confusion and make for a better work environment and information service.

There are several excellent resources on the MBTI and Gardner's multiple intelligences. The reader is encouraged to consult the resources section for further in-depth reading. What follows is a generalized account of each type in the MBTI.

How a person prefers to take in information falls within the *introvert* and *extravert* categories. The introvert is a self-learner who works best alone, likes quiet and may prefer to have communication in writing. Its counterpart, the extravert, needs people to learn through the exchange of information. Extraverts typically prefer to receive and send communication verbally.

Gathering information may be done systematically, which is the *sensing* type's preference, while the *intuitive* type prefers to rely on impressions or "gut feeling." Sensing types also like an established way of doing things. They tend to work steadily and are careful about facts. Intuitive types dislike doing the same thing, tend to work in bursts, are known to leap to conclusions and like to ask why things are as they are.

Decision making has the preferences of *thinking* and *feeling* types. Thinking types tend to be detached, logical and objective and respond well to ideas. This focus on ideas and the tendency toward detachment means that thinking types may hurt people's feelings and not realize it. Those who score high on *feeling* typically like harmony and work toward it, respond to values as much as thought and enjoy pleasing people.

Finally, the lifestyle type of *judging* is planned and organized, dislikes interruptions, and wants only the essentials to begin. *Perceiving* types are much more spontaneous and flexible and may start projects but not finish them.

Table 2.2 is a brief account of the MBTI types discussed in this section.

This is a brief overview of the MBTI; if you would like an in-depth account of the Type Indicator, there are a number of books and other resources available. Please check the resources section at the end of this book for a brief bibliography.

The MBTI tells us how we prefer to process information, while Gardner's theory of multiple intelligences (1983, 1993, 1999) tells us where our cognitive strengths lie. There are nine basic intelligences, ten if you consider linguistic (oral and written) as two separate intelligences. Table 2.3 lists each with a brief description. The resources section lists several resources if you are interested in an in-depth study. As with the MBTI, the following are generalizations of Gardner's multiple intelligences and used for illustrative purposes only.

Intake of information	Introvert	Self-learner Works best alone
	Extravert	Needs people to learn Prefers verbal information
Data gathering	Sensing	Systematic Established way of doing things
	Intuitive	Relies on impressions Dislikes routine
Decision making	Thinking	Logical and objective Detached
	Feeling	Likes harmony Enjoys pleasing people
Lifestyle	Judging	Planned and organized Dislikes interruptions
	Perceiving	Spontaneous Flexible

Table 2.2   Synthesis of MBTI Types

The *linguistic* intelligence is seen in a mastery and love of language and words. Gardner considers the two types of linguistic intelligence, oral and written, as one; I think it is helpful to separate these. Some people are excellent orators and have less ability with the written word and vice versa. It is a rare individual who is gifted in both.

Logical-mathematical is displayed though assessing objects and abstractions and discerning their relationships. Scientists and mathematicians have this intelligence, as do philosophers.

Linguistic (oral and written)	Mastery and love of language
Logical-mathematical	Assessing objects and abstractions
Musical	Composing, performing
Spatial	Visual perception
Bodily-kinesthetic	Control and orchestrate body motions
Intrapersonal	Self-aware
Interpersonal	Aware of other's moods and feelings
Naturalist	Aware of surroundings
Existential	Spiritual awareness

Table 2.3   Gardner's Multiple Intelligences

Competence in composing, performing, listening and discerning are traits of the *musical* intelligence, while the ability to perceive the visual world and recreate visual experiences are traits of those with *spatial* intelligence.

Dancers, athletes and actors demonstrate the *bodily-kinesthetic* intelligence through their ability to control and orchestrate body motions.

"Self-awareness" is another term for the traits of the *intrapersonal* intelligence, someone who is able to determine moods, feelings, and other mental states in him- or herself. The *interpersonal* intelligence's strength is in determining moods, feelings and mental states of others.

Naturalist intelligence is demonstrated through recognizing and categorizing natural objects. Finally, the *existential* intelligence captures and ponders the fundamental questions of existence. Existential intelligence is another way of describing those with spiritual gifts and interests.

Having provided a cursory introduction, we can begin to apply learning theory to our quest for customized service. One tool I use is an instrument based on MBTI and Gardner's theories that gives me a general idea of how my client prefers to receive and use information. The instrument is best used in conjunction with a short interview. For true accuracy of learning style type, I encourage the use of the MBTI available through Consulting Psychologists Press. Please see the resources section for contact information.

To summarize, the MBTI helps us to understand information processing traits while Gardner's theory enables us to fine-tune our understanding of those traits.

What is the last but equally important piece in the process— what will this information package be used for? Put together, these pieces tell us what information is needed, how it will be processed and how it will be applied. The result is the information product that is the perfect fit for that client in that situation. It is the customized fit available only through a professional's skills of recursive diagnosis and treatment.

Interviewing Techniques

The next chapter expands on the necessity of people skills for success in the information field, but for now let's agree that in order to assess who a person is, what his or her learning preferences are and what they plan to do with your product requires the ability to hold a conversation with a stranger or near-stranger. And that's what interviews should be—conversations, not inquisitions.

Reference librarians are some of my favorite people in the profession. I especially admire the superbly talented ones who can gently persuade a patron to confide that he's looking for information on abortion when his first request was for a book on family health—all in the space of about two minutes. I have watched these types of exchanges enough to know it is a process that leaves the client with the clear understanding that what our profession is really about is matching the right information in the right format with the right client. We are professionals who view our clients' needs as more important than our personal views. Inasmuch as it is possible, we remain neutral regarding our clients' requests.

Starting the Interview

Have an idea of what you want to know. Are you charged with providing information services to a group or an individual? Do you need to design an information system, or are you conducting research on a specific subject? Just as it's important to understand how your client's situation affects his or her information request, so you must understand the situation you're operating in and pose your questions accordingly.

After you've obtained the specific individual information, ask neutral, open-ended questions. Try to avoid leading questions, such as, "What part of your current incompetent, worthless information system do you dislike most?" Write out the questions in advance, but let the client's answers direct your follow up questions. Don't be compelled to stick to the script—

this is interviewing, not survey work. A list of sample interview questions is found in the resources section. The questions are labeled by potential use: "General" means you would use the answers to provide data for a general client profile; "Information Need" questions are used to determine what gaps need to be addressed. "Information Flow" questions are designed to help you uncover who talks to whom, a very necessary part of uncovering a great organizational resource, the community of practice. The questions in the resources section are just suggestions to be used as you develop your own interview instrument.

Observations

Observation methodology comes from the field of anthropology. Its challenge is to see what happens, not what is staged for your benefit. I find that dressing within the corporate culture's style and staying quiet helps me to blend in and eventually have my presence forgotten. I also take lots and lots of notes that I download and fill out when I get home in order to accurately recreate the activities, actions and interactions that I witnessed.

Observations are most useful for finding out what information the client really finds useful, rather than relying on their interview answers that may list some reading materials that they never look at but feel they should. Again, we don't judge our clients for what they should or shouldn't read—or what they do or don't read. Knowing what content they find useful and what style of presentation captures their attention satisfies our professional curiosity and makes it possible for us to help them get the information they need but haven't had time for.

Observations are also useful for uncovering the corporate culture. Some of this is revealed in the office décor, some of it is seen in the dress code. Who talks to whom, the vocabulary that's used and the stories that are told and retold; these are important pieces that help the information professional sketch a corporate profile to which his or her services will be tailored. These pieces cannot be located in a survey and rarely surface during an interview.

Putting the Pieces Together

You have your observation notes and interview answers— now what? In some cases the answer will be clear ("We need a database that will manage all client accounts"); in others, one problem may be stated ("Organize the corporate library") but your notes will uncover additional problems lurking in the background, such as severe retrieval limitations within the central filing system. It's your professional responsibility to inform the client when you find problems in addition to what you were called in for, but don't be surprised if they pass on your suggestion to address them immediately. Be patient, and monitor the situation as best you can. All you can do is provide the professional assessment; it's up to the client whether to heed your advice.

Your notes will tell you what roles each employee has. This is very important when designing a customized information delivery service, since an employee's role will directly affect what content is important. It may seem obvious to state that the finance department will want to read *Forbes* and *The Wall Street Journal*, but who among them has the accounting specialization?

Which part of accounting do they specialize in? Who handles investments? It doesn't take long to identify the subspecialties within a single department; imagine how many subspecialties you could uncover in the overall organization. This level of specificity is necessary to provide the value-added services that not only make your clients' lives easier but help their company transition into a true learning organization.

High quality service takes time to develop. If your client lets you in to interview and observe, be respectful of the risk your client is taking in terms of industrial information and confidentiality. Be respectful of their privacy and sensitive information. Treat everyone with dignity.

The bottom line on diagnosis and analysis is that they are done to help you understand your client. You should express your professional concerns but refrain from judgment that leads to ridicule. Different learning styles are just that—different—and not inherently better than others. As information professionals, we celebrate diversity on all levels and welcome the opportunity to be of service to all.

Notes

1. Wilson, P. (1977). *Public knowledge and private ignorance.* Westport, CT: Greenwood Press.

Chapter 3
Learning to Learn Together

P eople often say to me, "I'd love to do what you do—I like to work by myself." That's like saying, "I want to be a librarian because I love books." Books are meaningless unless they are read and enjoyed by people, which is why good librarians are people persons. By the same token, successful information professionals have to be people persons on both the micro and macro levels. They must be skilled at reading their client's environment and organizational objectives, both of which are subject to constant change. Because we work by contract, our job security rests in our ability to deliver quality service and a product that demonstrates our understanding and appreciation of our client's unique requirements. It's hard to come up with those skills if you lack the people skills needed to establish a professional relationship with your client.

Granted, I am able to do some things by myself. Other projects may require forming a team with other professionals. Regardless of whether it's a solo or group project, everything I do is based on an assessment of my client's needs and with the understanding that it will be used and critiqued and strengthened by others. Whether I am serving on-site or in my home office, I am engaged in a collaborative relationship. Successful collaborative relationships are based on the idea that people are the most important factor in the information service and that collectively we can produce better quality than by working alone.

Success in collaboration is the ability to park your ego at the door and put the needs of the group ahead of any individual. That's not to say you shouldn't dig in your heels and fight for what you believe. It does mean that you must view others' ideas with respect and be willing to compromise in order to achieve the greater good. It also means that communication skills are important, particularly when face-to-face contact is not always possible.

Technology is what allows me to work miles away from my clients. It's what gives me a "virtual" presence—more than one client has said "it's just like you were in our building" in reference to my responsiveness via email or telephone. A good description for how I work is "autonomous, not isolated."

Despite my fondness for technology and remote connections, I also spend a certain amount of time in face-to-face contact with clients. Depending on the geographic distance involved, that may be once a week, month, or year. The face-to-face interaction is very important because it allows me to see firsthand what is new in my client's world. As much as it is appropriate and possible, I incorporate those changes into the services I deliver. I also use this time to talk informally with as many employees as possible. It's through these casual conversations that I gather valuable data on change in roles, corporate objectives and other factors that have an impact on the level of professional service I provide. It also gives me a chance to build relationships that are the foundation for working collaboratively.

Learning Styles at Work

In the last chapter we briefly discussed the Myers-Briggs Type Indicator (MBTI) and Howard Gardner's theory of multiple intelligences. These are just two of the frames of reference that I use in my work but are enough for this chapter's exercise of examining how different learning styles can work together effectively. Again, please read these as the general examples they are intended to be.

Our previous discussion of the MBTI made it clear that the two types within each category are opposites. Depending on the combination of preferences, the resulting combination can be a natural complement to another's learning style, or it may be like mixing oil and water. We know that introverts ("I") prefer to be self-learners and take in information on their own, while extraverts ("E") prefer to give and receive information verbally. Imagine a strong *I* sharing an office with a strong *E* and you can see disaster looming. It doesn't have to be a foregone conclusion if each person makes an effort to accommodate the other's learning style. When you're in a foreign country it helps to at least try to speak the native language. It's not so different when opposite learning styles are working together.

As an *INTJ* (Introvert/Intuitive/Thinking/Judging), I work best with extraverts when I remember to speak up and project enthusiasm. If I'm lucky, my *E* colleague will make allowance for my learning style by writing out her ideas first and giving me time to reflect. Each of us has to understand that what is natural to one is unfamiliar to the other and may even be difficult to attempt. Humor and patience are great resources during this transition time.

Sensing ("S") types are systematic while intuitive ("N") types rely on impressions for data gathering, but both can work together if S learns to state the big idea first and resist the urge to dismiss immediately N's sketchy plans. As an N, I should work out the details ahead of time and state the problem explicitly before presenting it to my S colleague. Chances are the communication will flow more smoothly and the ideas will be better accepted.

The logical, objective thinking ("T") types' focus on ideas can unintentionally offend others, and feeling types ("F") are possibly the most easily wounded. It's not that we Ts are bereft of feelings, we just value the more concrete over the subjective. Feelings in the workplace can be anathema to us; fortunately, Fs are better at being empathetic and may show us some mercy while we learn to adapt. Concrete efforts that Ts can make include mentioning points of agreement and stating concern for the people involved. Fs do well to address the task first when working with Ts, arrange comments logically and use assertive communication skills.

As with any learning style, certain combinations are strengths in some circumstances, while in other situations they can be a hindrance. I suspect that the majority of the library profession has "TJ" (Thinking/Judging) in their MBTI, which works well for our ability to organize and think logically. However, it can be a hindrance if we let it prevent new ways of thinking and experiencing. As a J (Judging) working with Ps (Perceiving), I have to be flexible, open to new ideas and willing to readjust my thinking. This has become easier over the years, but it does take practice. Ps, on the other hand, can make our load a bit easier if they plan ahead, make decisions and try to structure their conversation.

Gardner's theory of multiple intelligences provides us with an appreciation of individual cognitive strengths. Although these may influence the type of information a person may prefer, processing preferences remain in the realm of the MBTI.

Acknowledging and valuing multiple intelligences means we appreciate a diversity of cognitive skills in the workplace, and we recognize the particular skills of personal and interpersonal skills. Although we appreciate this diversity, learning styles are not an excuse for bad behavior ("What do you expect out of a TJ?"), nor are they to be accommodated at the expense of others. A person strong in the naturalistic intelligence may have to give up the office plant on behalf of the coworker with serious allergies. Musically inclined coworkers may have to constrain their favorite passion during their lunch breaks and after work. So, celebrate and utilize the various intellectual strengths dealt to you—just don't let any of them become barriers to collaboration.

The implications of learning styles for the information professional should be clear. We have to be aware of the many differences possible in any client organization, and we should allow for these differences in the services we render. We can use this knowledge as we conduct our observations and integrate them into our recommendations. Physical layout, furniture, directional signs, formats and types of materials as well as specific services are all affected by learning styles and intelligences. Once we're aware of our clients' preferences, we have the responsibility to design our presentations accordingly. After all, our chief objective is to provide a seamless interface between the user and the information.

Situations and Roles

Information needs are based on situation and role. My current situation explains why I need driving directions to the Wichita, Kansas, airport while my role as an information professional dictates why I have travel plans. One is immediate and the other is part of a larger picture of who I am and, consequently, what dictates my information needs. Day-to-day, I am more likely to filter information based on my role first, then my situation. The exceptions to this are when a situation is urgent, such as when I need a new printer cartridge. Even then, my role as business owner kicks in to determine where I can get the best deal and to remember to use the corporate credit card.

People process information differently based on their current role. The information needs of a parent whose oldest child is two years old are much different than the information needs of parent whose youngest child just turned twenty-two. Both parents may work in the same field, maybe even for the same company. Their work roles may be alike enough to filter professional information similarly, but I'm willing to bet that their leisure reading is significantly different. For one, the parent of the two-year-old is not likely to have much leisure time, and I would venture that what little reading she can work in is in short doses. The parent of the twenty-two-year-old may be reading up on childcare, but possibly as a refresher course in anticipation of the first grandchild. If, like me, you don't have children, chances are the diaper ads on TV don't trip your radar. But if, like me, you live in a menagerie of animals that adopted you, cat and dog food commercials are more likely to catch your attention. The point is that information is more apt to grab our attention when it relates to one of our roles. Information that does not have a clear relation may become invisible. A good information professional will help her client obtain both the visible and the invisible information, particularly when the latter has the potential to make a significant difference in the client's life.

Collaboration

In chapter 2, we talked briefly about Harlan Cleveland's characteristics of information. The bottom line is that information is unlike any of the physical resources we are most familiar with. The Information Age has ushered in some radical ideas, including the concept of simultaneous ownership. If I know a fact and you know a fact we both "own" the same fact, which is somewhat akin to each of us owning the same model of computer or car or television set. What drives the value of physical goods and information differs to an extent. Physical goods have market value based on availability and demand. For example, in the mid 1990s there was a rage first among pre-teens and later among middle-aged adults (who should have known better) for collecting small, stuffed toys called Beanie Babies. Scarcity of certain types drove the prices up as high as several hundred dollars apiece. Stores would sell out within hours of receiving their shipments. The popularity and value of what should have been a five-dollar toy was driven in large part by the need to obtain the unobtainable. Once the manufacturer finally caught up to consumer demand, the fad ended and prices dropped to their retail levels.

Information at the right—and for a remarkably short period of—time has value like the Beanie Babies that went for hundreds more than their suggested retail price. Being the first to know a juicy piece of gossip has a psychological effect similar to those who could "score" the elusive Tabasco (Bull) Beanie Baby. Likewise, having legitimate financial information at the right time could make one wealthy through a timely investment. "Old" financial news (anything older than fifteen minutes, according to traditional wisdom) could have the opposite effect. Information that meets a specific, urgent need—such as best practices for treating a serious medical condition—has distinct value to the seeker. Each of these circumstances reflects the importance of situation, role and user in determining value. And although one Tabasco Beanie Baby can be owned in only one place at a time, any number of people can have access to gossip, financial news or medical information.

If information is readily available and few people have control over it for the briefest of moments, then it stands to reason that the rules have changed regarding the workplace. When we saw information hoarding as the ticket for power, we adopted organizational structures that ensured a competitive environment and strict controls over who had access to what. Those at the upper end of the hierarchy tended to have access while those toward the bottom would have access to only what the people at the top were comfortable with them knowing. If those at the top of the hierarchy were insecure, those at the bottom would have little access, regardless of how much easier their jobs would be with freer access.

In short, we developed systems that rewarded competitiveness and punished collegiality and collaboration. This antiquated system is antithetical to what today's companies need to succeed. Companies have to be able to react quickly to rapidly changing environments, and that cannot be done if the old ways of information hoarding are in place. Enter the realm of collaboration, where coworkers willingly share ideas, develop and work on projects jointly, and celebrate the results as a team.

Harlan Cleveland taught us that information is an odd commodity in that the more it's used and the more people who have it the more valuable it becomes. Therefore, companies can rest assured that to share information openly and to train employees how to maximize their information use is to make a solid investment in the future.

Companies that make this kind of investment may find their employees taking charge of their own learning. It has been my experience that, regardless of the organization, most employees want to do a good job. Occasionally they seek out like-minded individuals who may or may not be part of their official department structure and form informal learning communities. Jean Lave and Etienne Wenger wrote about these groups, calling them term "communities of practice" (COPs) in the 1991 book *Situated Learning*. At the time, Lave and Wenger were both affiliated with the Institute for Research on Learning (IRL), which was founded in 1987 as a spin-off of Xerox's Palo Alto Research Center. The mission of IRL was to study how people learn. The fundamental finding was that learning is social and that it happens in groups.

The concept of COPs is founded on situated learning, which assumes that learning is a process of social participation. Situated learning takes place on two levels: the learner learns from others in order to fit in socially, and the social setting continues to serve as a learning environment after the novice has become an accepted member of the group. Situated learning sees the social process as an integral part to the group process of learning (Lave and Wenger, 1991). Situated learning is also considered the backbone of organizational learning.

An information professional should be aware of COPs in order to tap into their client's home-based, ongoing learning. Here are some COP characteristics to look for:

- They emerge of their own accord
- They are formed by people who are drawn to one another by a force that's both social and professional
- They collaborate directly
- Members use one another as sounding boards and teach each other
- They cannot be formed by decree
- They are easy to destroy
- They almost inevitably undermine formal structures and strictures and consequently may be seen as a threat by bureaucratically minded executives (Stewart, 1996)

To Stewart's list of characteristics we can add Etienne Wenger's traits of COPs:

- They have history
- They develop over time
- They can be defined in terms of the learning they do over time

- They have an enterprise but not an agenda
- They form around a value-adding "something-we're-all-doing"

Communities of practice are frequently overlooked because they do not follow the existing departmental lines. They have their own communications system and view traditional boundary lines as something to be crossed. Their motto could well be, "Information Wants to Be Free" (Stewart, 1996).

To summarize, communities of practice illustrate two key concepts of adult learning:

- Learning is social
- Learning happens on the job

Communities of practice should not be confused with teams charged with specific goals, although members of COPs may meet each other through this type of work. The information professional should be aware of both types of entities in order to provide accurate, customized services. The COPs will typically reflect a more diverse membership than project teams; however, both will have their share of information needs.

The Information Professional as a Team Member

At the beginning of this chapter I made the point that an information business may be a sole proprietorship, but it doesn't mean working alone. Information professionals are frequently called upon to work with members of a client's organization in order to achieve a specific project goal. The good news is that you're an outsider who has a neutral perspective on your client's information needs. The bad news is that you're an outsider who has no authority over other team members' actions (or lack thereof). How do you motivate when you have nothing to motivate with?

You learn the fine art of teamwork and leading from within. Granted, you have an added disadvantage of not having any say in who participates in the team, but you can make the best of it. The key is to understand what makes teams work effectively.

Teams work best if the project is planned carefully with the objectives clearly defined. Once the project's objectives are identified, team members are selected based on the roles that are needed to ensure a successful project. You look for individual skills that collectively form a strong unit. Some of these skills may be areas of expertise, some may be learning styles, and some may relate to the individual's personality and working style.

The team goes through several stages as it begins its work. The early stages are a time during which members clarify their role within the project objectives. This phase of uncertainty may present some conflict as members "jockey for position." In a best-case scenario, at this stage conflict is not only resolved but is used effectively as a learning opportunity and to develop the team's viewpoint, language and practices. There is no magic timeframe during which the team settles in and begins to work together effectively. In the worst-case scenario, it never happens.

Let's assume that the team you're assigned to has been carefully planned and has a clear agenda. It still has to function well and a key component for that is communication. This is easier said than done, for members of the same organization may use the same words but often have different meanings. An effort to clarify the vocabulary should be an early team activity. This will make it easier for each member to hear what others say—not only the words but the intended content. As the team's information expert it may fall upon you to act as "knowledge coordinator." You will need to draw on our profession's ability to understand a discipline or field by studying the vocabulary in context, and you may become the "translator" between disciplines. If you speak everyone's language, then you become a role model of collaboration. This is an excellent time to demonstrate your leadership and help keep the team running smoothly.

An understanding and appreciation of different learning styles and intelligences is helpful for any team. Different is not only OK, it has the potential to strengthen the team's ability to see different facets of a problem. Consequently, the team is better able to proactively solve what might have gone unnoticed until problems occurred.

The ability to communicate helps team members through conflict and handling change. Communication is not just articulating thoughts through a common vocabulary; it involves listening to what others say and checking to make sure what was heard was what the speaker intended. Communication is critical to the ongoing activities during the project and for writing the final report at the project's completion.

This chapter has shown us how we can use our knowledge of learning styles and multiple intelligences as we deliver information services to multiple clients. This knowledge helps us work effectively in teams. It also helps us demonstrate our client-centeredness. We understand how people look for information and therefore are more likely to deliver what they need and in the format they prefer. Our professional expertise is greatly enhanced when we add our understanding of how roles affect a person's ability to view and use information. Understanding our clients and proactively providing information we have filtered using their lens is the apex of our profession.

Chapter 4

Supporting Creation and Use

One of the joys of the information profession is having a hand in the creation of information, or what academicians call "contributing to the knowledge base." Higher education might like to think it has the knowledge creation market cornered, but today's businesses understand that their employees are creating knowledge with every project they undertake. They also know that to capitalize on their intellectual capital means an increased bottom line.

Information has a lifecycle that encompasses its creation, use, storage followed by retrieval for more use, which may involve re-creation, back to use, storage, retrieval, etc., until the final disposition of archival or discard is reached. Figure 4.1 illustrates this process. The lifecycle may be straightforward and linear but more often it is reiterative and very nonlinear.

Enter the Learning Organization

Learning organizations are those that make a concerted effort to manage information according to its lifecycle. Most organizations store and forget; learning organizations realize that they have created a valuable resource in every document their members have produced. More importantly, they put these resources to work, thus leveraging expensive commodities and contributing to their bottom line.

The foundation for a learning organization is a culture that is willing to examine what is known, question its assumptions

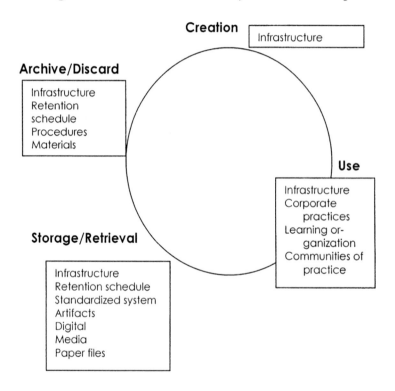

Figure 4.1   The Information Lifecycle

and grow from the experience. The term "learning organization" may appear to have become an overused buzzword, but it deserves recognition as a legitimate focus and goal. Adopting the practices of a learning organization is driven by economics. If you don't have to reinvent the wheel each time, eventually you begin to save on the initial outlay of intellectual capital. And if you're really good, you learn to sell your knowledge to others, further increasing your organization's capital.

Being able to use and reuse homegrown knowledge is the beginning of the learning organization. Businesses that recognize the inherent value in managing their information understand the necessity of devising a system that allows internally generated knowledge to be transparently created, used and shared.

What this means to the information professional is that learning organizations willing to capitalize on their intellectual capital have given us an professional opportunity. The coin of the learning organization realm is information—more specifically, it is information that can be readily accessed, used and stored for future use. To achieve that you need an information infrastructure—and to build a solid information infrastructure, you need an information professional.

Information professionals have a neutral view of their clients' information systems, which is to say they are not as inclined to be adversely influenced by internal politics as in-house employees might be. Information professionals have the ability to see the big picture and offer comprehensive services that ensure the best quality possible. We do this by building on the fundamentals that chapters 2 and 3 present, and we expand into system design. We look at what the client does now and we listen to understand where they want to go. Very few businesses have as their mission statement, "To shrink into insignificance and die a whimpering, premature death." Most businesses anticipate growth or at least want to be able to accommodate growth, and you can help them get there. Every information system has to anticipate the amount and type of data to be organized and the number of users who will access this tool. It must also take into account technology yet to be invented. We handle this challenge through a flexible design, by setting policies that focus on content rather than format, and we make provisions for converting data into new, appropriate formats.

Chapters 2 and 3 talk about getting to know one's client, and that applies no matter what size the client organization. We use a number of methodologies, including interviews, observations, document and artifact analysis, cultural understanding, and use of narrative to gather data that will lead to an accurate analysis. If you are working with an organization of more than forty employees, I recommend bringing in one or more professionals and forming a team to gather and analyze data. Two professionals can cover a large (more than 150 employees) work unit, but there is no sense in stretching the talent too thin. An initial site visit is standard when bidding on a project, so use your professional judgment when determining when to bring in additional professionals and how many the project needs.

Let's say the client wants to ensure compliance with records retention and accomplish this in a cost-effective manner. We use our needs assessment and diagnostic skills to determine key facts about the company and its employees, since we will need to start with the industry specifications for records retention and assess the client's current compliance levels. Understanding the current work practices helps pave the way for implementation of the new system. We want to avoid unnecessary turmoil in the implementation of a new system, and knowing how the employees will adapt to a new system allows us to know what stages need to be phased in and when.

A records retention system is actually an all-encompassing information system, because to be effective it will track information from its creation to final disposition. It is a good example to use for this book because in subsequent chapters we will address storing to retrieve (filing system and organization) and protecting for the future (corporate memory and archives).

A Case Study

Company DCD[1] is a retail establishment that employs sixty-seven full- and part-time workers. Federal and state employment and sales tax regulations drive its primary records retention requirements. Other employee-related requirements include payroll, insurance and accident reports. We can foresee that additional records management needs would include inventory control (sales, orders, returns). The company's employees are a diverse group of ages and education levels with a range of computer skills from novice to expert. As part of the records management compliance project, the management is willing to upgrade its present computer system and revamp its outdated paper filing system. The client would like to accomplish this within a year. However, the high probability of adding inventory control to the system causes us to negotiate for an eighteen-month timeframe. Still, this will be a fast-track, complex project with the potential for unforeseen delays. We ask that the contractual agreement include frequent progress reports so the client will know whether the project is on target and to work with us to troubleshoot bottleneck areas.

Our initial consultation gave us the brief background described in the preceding paragraph. Now we need a more thorough understanding of the corporate environment and organizational practices. We decide to conduct observations and interviews and should be able to accomplish this in a three-day site visit.

My first rule of observation work is to dress so that you can blend in easily. Our initial consultation gave us an idea of the style of dress affected by employees and customers, and we dress accordingly. We also agree to restrict our conversations to the interviews, during which we may ask for clarification or confirmation of our observations. While the research community understands that no qualitative research method is unbiased, we do try to be as inconspicuous and least disruptive to the typical routine as possible.

Our contract states that we will keep all company information confidential. This is a very important component of contract work. We have to have our clients' trust to provide good service and to ensure repeat business. Our clients take risks in making sensitive information available to us, and we have to respect their privacy. Consequently, we guard our notes and practice appropriate records management of our own in order to protect our clients.

During our three-day site visit we plan to interview upper and middle management, observe employee practices on the sales floor, receiving and stocking, and gain an understanding of the returns process. We want to look at the current computer system and existing paper filing system. The site visit days will be long; we will be spending our evenings typing up our observational and interview data to ensure timely, accurate notes.

We will begin the data analysis back at the office, and we let the data tell us the company's story. Although we want to state clearly and in full detail what processes are in place, we also want to remain open to the unanticipated findings that will emerge (if we let them). We will detail the existing system and compare this against the current practices. An information flow map will help us identify where redundancy decreases efficiency and we can brainstorm how to solve those efficiency gaps. We will also want to look at our data within the framework of the information lifecycle.

Chapter 2 discusses the diagnostic process, and this type of project calls for its organizational counterpart of analysis. The process is quite similar; where one would diagnose an individual's information needs, one analyzes an organization. An information answer is provided as a prescription to an individual; groups receive recommendations. An individual receives the information "treatment"; the organization has its recommendation implemented. Both the individual and group information services are evaluated. When working with an organization, your evaluation steps should be outlined in your contract. As the project progresses you should be using formative evaluation to guide the project and, upon its completion, provide a summative evaluation.

Our first data analysis of the Company DCD project provides guidelines for evaluation in that we have decided to group the information needs by department function. We have been told that the primary force behind records compliance is state and federal tax law, but limiting our focus on those areas reduces our ability to provide services in accordance with our professional ethics. Any change to an information system has to be considerate of the other components. Therefore, although we are charged with addressing one component, it must work smoothly with the rest of the information infrastructure. We cannot be certain that will be the case unless we look at and analyze the entire system.

Tables 4.1 and 4.2 show the areas of primary focus and secondary concern, respectively. The reader will no doubt recognize the inherent relationship between the two system areas. The value common to both is employees, since we want to have records of who ordered, received, sold and/or shipped inventory.

Finance/Human Resources					
Payroll	Employee Records	Benefits	Marketing	Accounts Payable	Accounts Receivable

Table 4.1   Company DCD Areas of Primary Focus

Retail/Inventory Control					
Orders	Receiving	Stock	Sales	Returns	Shipping

Table 4.2   Company DCD Areas of Secondary Focus

Our data for the Company DCD project have further uses. We need to analyze these to determine roles, information needs and business processes. We should be aware of areas that need improvement, even though they were not mentioned as part of the original project. For example, I once did a study of an organization with the purpose of establishing a corporate library. In the process of a needs analysis I discovered that the existing filing system was impossible to use, even for ten-year veterans who presumably knew where things were supposed to be. Even if the client does not want to address anything outside of the contractual agreement, it is your professional responsibility to be forthcoming with your assessment.

Looking for what doesn't work isn't all that difficult. Looking for what does work takes a little practice and is well worth the effort. You want to build on the organization's strengths, and every organization is usually doing at least one thing right.

Data Analysis

If you let it, the data will tell you everything you need to know to design the best information system for the Company DCD project. Just like our earlier discussion on how to diagnose an individual's information needs, we analyze the organization's information needs using the framework of the *who, how* and *what*. Who asks, "Who are the gatekeepers?" that is, who controls or is in a position to control key information?

Other "who" questions:

- "Who talks to whom?"
- "Who requests what from whom?"
- "Who uses what information, and who else needs it?"

Answers to these may uncover gaps in the current processes that, once solved, increase efficiency. The "who" questions help us understand departments and divisions and reveal cross-department relationships. This is where communities of practice are found, and we see it in the informal conversations among and between coworkers.

In chapter 2, we said that "how" questions pertain to individuals' information processing styles. In the corporate setting, researching how people obtain and use information helps us understand business practices.

"How" questions can be tricky because they often begin with "what." For example:

- "What information do people use and *how* do they obtain it?"
- "What do people do when they can't get the information they need?" has the understood clause, "and *how* do they react?"

"How" is possibly the biggest portion of the corporate information analysis process. We want to customize our product to the client's needs, and to do that for an organization we have to understand both individual and company-wide information practices. Other questions I recommend using during data analysis:

- "What do people do with the information they receive?"
  - o "How do they process it?"
  - o "Where do they keep it?"
  - o "Who do they send it to?"
  - o "How do they store it?"
  - o "How do they apply it?"

The "what" questions for the individual seek to answer: "what does the client want to do with this information?" It may seem obvious in an organizational setting that the business wants to increase efficiency in order to increase profits. But does it really? Is that your assumption, or did you ask the owners and management about their goals? If you are working with a for-profit enterprise, efficiency and profits are important considerations. To provide the best level of service, ask your client for their vision, mission and goals document. This can help clarify the information system priorities.

During the Company DCD project we will practice the recursive quality of diagnosis in that we will present our findings to management and employees for their feedback. This continual dialogue is necessary to ensure our work will fit their needs, and it builds ownership that facilitates implementation. Our final recommendations are a combination of our professional judgment based on the data analysis and the DCD group's input. Only by working collegially can we develop an appropriate system in terms of hardware, software and peopleware—the latter including the policy changes needed for more efficient procedures.

Notes

1. Company DCD is a fictitious composite of client organizations. Any resemblance to an actual company, past or present, is pure coincidence.

Chapter 5

Facilitating Organizational Learning

What does an information infrastructure contribute to a learning organization? Let me give you a hint—it's more than a nice place to save electronic files but less than the organizational culture. In other words, a properly designed information system will contribute significantly to an organization's ability to learn, but it isn't everything. The organization has to have a culture of learning for any information system to be effective.

A culture of learning is the willingness to open up the books to peers and hear them say, "Here—try this" in response to a problem. It's the ability to share information freely, knowing that there is no reward for claiming solo credit but plenty of rewards for evidence of solid teamwork. As information professionals, you and I do not have the ability to convince organizations to adopt a culture of learning. We do, however, have the opportunity to educate when we can and celebrate when we are working with true learning organizations.

When we talked about setting up an information infrastructure in chapter 4, we used the model of the learning organization as justification to provide this valuable service. We also talked about individual learning styles or information processing preferences in chapter 3. Now it's time to look at learning at the organizational level and its counterpart called knowledge management—a combination of technology and people, of infrastructure and culture.

Figure 5.1 illustrates the continuum of information infrastructure services available. The continuum is drawn at an upward slope to demonstrate hierarchy of service.

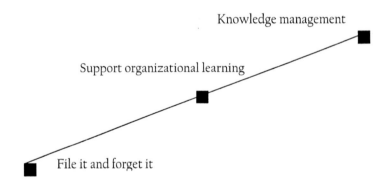

Figure 5.1   Information Infrastructure Services Continuum

The Company DCD project from the previous chapter is an example of being asked to work on one component of an information infrastructure when the real need is to have a comprehensive information system that addresses larger needs, such as organizational learning and knowledge management. Let's operate under the assumption that the Company DCD management understands and values the need to improve other parts of their information infrastructure and are now eagerly anticipating a system that will support their long-term goal of knowledge management. We can congratulate ourselves on having the vision to base the first part of the Company DCD project on the organization's vision, mission and goals. This supplies us with the framework to identify and codify the intellectual capital that exists with the Company DCD organization.

We may want to revisit the data from the first phase of the Company DCD project to identify the company's resources and capabilities in the knowledge management context. For example, how would we rate Company DCD's ability to respond to market demands? How well are employees trained on customer service, records keeping and other critical processes? How much informal learning takes place, and how well does management encourage it? Did we identify the communities of practice as a key resource at Company DCD? These informal groups join together to problem solve and share best practices in an organization and are considered by many to be the backbone of organizational learning. We can recommend that management encourage their existence by eliminating barriers to information and providing support.

Learning Organization Defined

Before we move from improving records retention compliance to the more complex issue of knowledge management, I propropose that we take an inventory of what it means to be a learning organization. Learning at the organizational level is different from learning at the individual level. We can start to understand this concept by looking at what we know about individual learning, research that has come to us from the fields of biology, psychology and education.

How an individual learns is different than how organizations learn. Organizational learning requires a group "mind," formed from the organization's vision and mission and influenced by its culture or belief system. Individual learning is explained through cognitive science, which emphasizes the importance of symbols and language. Organizations have their sets of symbols too—logos, mottos, office décor and dress code are all part of the corporate language. Each organization has its own vocabulary derived from its industry and peppered with allusions to company lore or anecdotes. These references become part of the company myth and are repeated long after the original incident occurred. To know the "company speak" is to demonstrate one's standing, and the more "in" terms one uses, the more one is perceived to be a part of the accepted crowd.

The influence of organizational culture clearly demonstrates the social aspect of learning, and it is this social aspect that partially accounts for the failure of the network (computer) analogy to describe organizational learning. Computer network theory focuses on the technology first and data second, and we already know that learning is more than a biological function. The social factors of environment and culture also play a role. Therefore, it is the social aspect of learning that is as important to groups as it is to individuals.

Despite the differences between individual and group learning, there is one factor held in common that influences the information professional's work. That factor is communication and it requires a shared language. In an organization, meaning is often constructed by consensus. It is the rare organization that does not have its own vocabulary derived from historical anecdotes and existing business practices. This language is a type of shorthand, used for expediency and to demonstrate one's standing in the corporate culture.

This chapter is about the learning organization and the opportunities for service they provide to information professionals. We already know the importance of learning as a social action, and the role of a shared vocabulary for clear communication. Let's add to our professional knowledge base through a better understanding of a learning organization's characteristics.

The majority of literature regarding learning organizations was developed by the field of business management, which saw organizational learning as a way to increase an organization's efficiency and profitability. However, what "organizational learning" means to the business world varies within the literature. Some definitions are as simplistic as saying a learning organization is "skilled at creating, acquiring, and transferring knowledge, and at modifying its behavior to reflect new knowledge and insights" (Garvin, 1993); others are more in-depth, such as this from Gephart et al. (1996):

> A learning organization is an organization that has an enhanced capacity to learn, adapt, and change. It is an organization in which learning processes are analyzed, monitored, developed, managed, and aligned with improvement and innovation goals. Its vision, strategy, leaders, values, structures, systems, processes, and practices all work to foster people's learning and development and to accelerate systems-level learning.

For the purposes of our work, it is helpful to know that organizational learning is more than a reactive response to new information. A true learning organization takes the time to learn ahead of time as well as reflect on its new knowledge through critical thinking skills. T. A. Stewart (2001) mentions the "peer assist" that some companies seek before beginning a new project. These are facilitated meetings held with your peers, those who have done what you intend to do, during which you ask them to share specific information pertaining to your proposed project. Another means of organizational learning is the "after-action review" or "debriefing" that involves answering these questions:

- What was supposed to happen?
- What actually happened?
- Why is there a difference?
- What can we learn from this and do differently? (Stewart, 2001, p. 166)

Companies that routinely practice debriefings and log their answers are on their way to becoming true learning organizations.

Like most things related to the information field, it's not a question of "or" but of "and" when we have two or more facets to a situation. The focus on learning at the group level does not preclude the interest in learning at the individual level. Gephart et al. (1996) sees individual learning as a necessary foundation to team or group learning and organizational learning. Through Gephart's model, we see the continuum of learning, starting with the individual and branching out to learning at the systems level, knowledge generation and sharing. Key to Gephart's model is the need for critical, systemic thinking, a culture of learning, a spirit of flexibility and experimentation, and people-centeredness.

As mentioned earlier, the information professional must be aware of communities of practice (COPs) as the needs assessment is conducted. COPs won't show up on the organizational chart but can be powerful sources of information and "how things are done." Wenger and Lave's theory says that learning is social and that it happens on the job. What kind of information system can we develop that will support organizational learning? If we look at the Company DCD project, we find that we already know where data is stored, who has what information and who uses it, and, more importantly, how it could be used and by whom.

The system that facilitates information creation and use and manages knowledge has these characteristics:

- *Ease of access.* Users find it so easy to use that they keep the system going and traditional barriers to information creation and access are removed.
- *User-based rules for permissions.* Users decide who should have access to what information and who should be responsible for updates.
- *Ability to capture the "fuzzy" knowledge.* Again, the system is so easy to use that user input of atypical information is encouraged and accommodated.

Individual learning theories are incapable of providing an adequate framework for understanding and managing organizational information processing. The communities of practice theory—the documented discovery that the foundation of organizational learning occurs in informal groups—is one framework that is suitable for use in examining how an organization learns. Information professionals can use this knowledge to help their client organizations become learning organizations through better information management.

Knowledge Management

In the first phase of the Company DCD project, we mapped out who talked with whom, who requested what information from whom, and what each party did with that information. We can build on this to map Company DCD's knowledge assets, which in turn will help the company "prioritize and focus its learning experiences" (Zack, 1999, p. 129). The DCD data contains the inventory that will allow us to make a knowledge map. This map demonstrates the types of knowledge located and illustrates other knowledge resources. It documents how knowledge flows within the organization and what formal and informal teams exist. It also shows impediments to knowledge sharing, impediments that can threaten the objectives of the information management project.

Greengard (1998) advises that companies interested in adopting knowledge management practices begin by eliminating three culturally-related barriers to knowledge management:

1. People are usually not inclined to share their brightest ideas.

2. People refuse to rely on others' ideas because doing so might make them seem less knowledgeable and more dependent on others.
3. People see themselves as experts and refuse collaboration.

Knowledge management barrier elimination begins with a three-part strategy for adopting knowledge management. First, management must provide leadership by obtaining and demonstrating an understanding of the importance of knowledge management. We have already established that the management of Company DCD is committed to developing an information infrastructure that includes knowledge management. Also needed from management are policies that underscore this commitment and an organizational culture that fosters collegial sharing of information. A second strategy is to form cross-functional teams to outline knowledge and plan a knowledge management program. This is where the communities of practice (COPs) we identified in the initial needs assessment can be particularly helpful. Tap into those informal information-rich networks and you've also tapped into the greater portion of the organization's knowledge. Finally, our portion of the Company DCD project addresses the third strategy of establishing a system for the collection and dissemination of information. Only after these three strategies are complete should the knowledge management technology be introduced.

The third component of Greengard's strategy holds the opportunity for the information professional to provide professional services. We can help companies who want to practice knowledge management understand the nature of information, particularly its characteristics of expandability, compressibility, substitutability, transportability, diffusiveness and "share-ability." Although there is no one definitive description of knowledge management, most experts would agree that it is not synonymous with technology and does in fact require a shift in how an organization uses and values information. Information professionals can help their clients make that transition.

Chapter 6
Storing to Retrieve

B y now we have a pretty good idea of what it takes to build a client relationship, one that lets us become acquainted, build trust, ask questions and poke around our client's workplace. We know how to design a system that allows for the creation of information, and we have learned to capitalize opportunities that lead our clients to adopting practices that support organizational learning. Now it's time to concentrate on managing the information our clients have created, including that which is no longer needed at their fingertips.

Chapter 4 introduces the concept of the information cycle (see figure 4.1) and how to analyze an organization's information needs. We have helped a fictitious company build an information infrastructure that supports information creation and use; now it is time to help them develop a system that will provide the complementary component of information retrieval. The ability to retrieve is an essential element of a knowledge management system.

Too often, storage of information is more of an exercise in "file it and forget it" than it is a process of storing to retrieve.

Done properly, information can be easily stored and used a number of times before reaching its final disposition. This is where learning takes place.

Our original assessment told us a number of things about our client company: what the organization's vision, mission and goals are; the corporate culture that influences how information

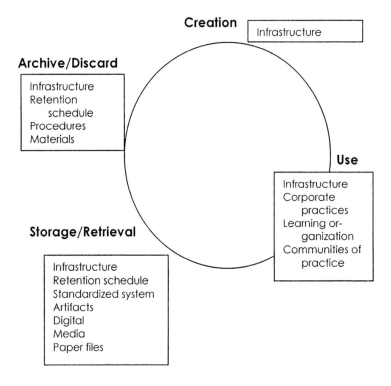

Figure 6.1   The Information Lifecycle

is processed; and the circumstances under which information is created and used. Since we know those vital pieces, we can design a system that continues to support our client's way of doing business.

The Company DCD project began with the goal of designing a system that would enable the company to achieve compliance with records retention for their industry. Because no part of an information system should be designed in isolation, we saw how it might be beneficial for the company to consider alterations to the overall system to facilitate information access and use. This would in turn support their efforts to be a learning organization. The component of storing to retrieve addresses issues of records retention and support for knowledge management.

Framework of System Design

Our background in situational learning (communities of practice) as applied to the Company DCD data analysis indicate the potential circumstances in which a document might need to be recovered. These situations are based on the groups of information use that we identified in the initial data analysis. We saw the overall organization having two main sections, finance and human resources and retail and inventory. Within the first section, we have payroll, employee records, employee benefits, marketing, accounts payable and accounts receivable. In the second section, we have orders, receiving, stock, sales, returns and shipping. Having identified the main components is only the beginning. In order to design a system that supports retrieval, we need to know the *who, how* and *what* of information access.

By thinking about who will be accessing information, how they prefer to access it and what their circumstance of information use might be, we can streamline the process and thus reduce the potential for errors. Despite the diversity of users and circumstances of information use, we can develop a standardized system that utilizes descriptive terms that have meaning to the organization.

Component	Who	How	What
Payroll	Accountant	Computer	Issue checks
Orders	Accountant	Computer	Reconcile statements
	Manager	Computer	Sales projections
	Salesperson	Hardcopy of online confirmation	Answer customer inquiry

Table 6.1   Examples of Information Use

Retention Schedules

Applying the standardized system to the retention schedules is a simpler prospect than might be expected. If we can foresee day-to-day interactions with the company's information, we can foresee what will be valuable in the future. Having established a system customized to the company's culture, language, mission and goals, it's not much more of an effort to include a retention schedule and procedure in the retrieval system.

Retention schedules are a combination of internally imposed rules and external legal requirements. Sometimes the internally imposed rules may differ from legal requirements, but they can never be more lax than the legal requirements. The legal requirements stem from federal and state laws; they typically pertain to employees and taxes but may involve other indus-try-specific regulations. One example is an agricultural supply company that sells products such as fertilizer and herbicides. This company would be required to keep proof of their compli-ance with the law by retaining documents such as the receipt and sale of hazardous chemicals and the federal chemical license number of each purchaser.

Records with a legal mandate for retention also have a minimum timeframe associated during which reasonable efforts must be made to ensure the integrity of these records. Because each industry has its own unique requirements, I recommend that clients annually review their retention schedules with their legal counsel.

Retention schedules can save companies money through re-ducing employee costs of maintaining and retrieving files. They save company costs in the discovery phase of a lawsuit. Typi-cally, there is a time limit during which records must be pro-duced. If a good system exists, retrieval can be timely and accurate. Also, courts generally accept documentation of records that have been destroyed in compliance with legal requirements and according to the organization's written information policy. In other words, evidence can legally be destroyed under certain circumstances, but it must be within legal parameters and care-fully documented. Finally, retention schedules save money in storage fees. Rather than keeping everything "just in case," com-panies can reduce the amount of off-site storage routinely used each year.

In response to the corporate scandals of the early 2000s, the Corporate Fraud Accountability Act of 2002 was passed to safe-guard corporate documents. Among its provisions is this clause:

Imposes a fine and/or imprisonment of not more than twenty years for "whoever knowingly alters, destroys, mutilates, conceals, covers up, falsifies, or makes a false entry in any record, document, or tangible object with the intent to impede, obstruct, or influence" an investigation or proceeding by a federal department or agency or any case filed in bankruptcy. (HR 3763, Sarbanes-Oxley Act of 2002)

Clearly, a system that tracks an item from its creation to its final disposition is in order. Fortunately, records management is relatively simple to maintain through the type of standardized system we are developing for the Company DCD project.

Standardized Information Systems

The first rule of a standardized system is that all users in an organization use the same filing system, regardless of the format. Whether the item in question is a hardcopy file, a computer (digital) file or a document such as a video tape or DVD, it receives a file number based on its content. The file number indicates at a glance which department the item originated in, its main subject and, if desired, its subheading. A record of each item's existence is entered into a database, thus beginning a way to track each document from its creation to its final disposition. There are information management software packages that perform these functions, or a company can have a customized database developed. See the resources section for a list of companies that produce information or document management software.

The advantage to a standardized system is multifold. By starting a database entry at the time a document is created, access to that information moves beyond its sole creator and thus supports organizational learning. The document format is not at issue; because of its record in a database, coworkers can easily ascertain where the document is, who has it and how they can physically access it. A brief description of the document's content will tell them whether it is a good match for their information need.

The standardized system encompasses all files within a company, regardless of their physical location. Under this system there are no personal files; all information is corporate property. This decentralized, controlled system facilitates information use because of the database record. At the same time, it ensures needed files are kept where they need to be—at a worker's fingertips rather than in a centralized file room.

The standardized system also addresses the sticky issues of digital data and other formats that don't fit into traditional hardcopy files. The database acts as the access point, and other technologies work to track all formats of data.

For example, hardcopy files and corporate artifacts may be suitable for a bar coding system, which can quickly update the location of the item the identity of the borrower. Some companies utilize radio frequency identification (RFID) technology, which involves tiny radio circuit chips in the barcode. These chips are activated when a reader comes into range; they require no external energy source.

RFID has found a use in the livestock industry and bears mentioning because of the propensity of unknown technologies to quickly come into being and replace the industry standard. It wasn't very long ago that cassette tapes had a "gold standard" for archival quality; they have since been replaced by CD-ROMs which in turn are being replaced by DVDs. It may be that another format for documents will be invented, one that does not lend itself to our current ways of labeling and tracking. RFID may be a solution to a future dilemma.

Another advantage to the standardized system is its ability to document the organization's knowledge creation. Corporate knowledge creation is expensive, so the more you can reuse it, the better your bottom line. By tracking when documents are used and by whom, a company can track part of its learning process. The other part of the learning process involves individuals' participation, and the proper system can track that, too, by allowing references to email correspondence, scanned notes and other artifacts of collaboration to be stored in the standardized system.

The standardized system gives new life to documents that might otherwise be ignored when they are no longer receiving constant or frequent use. A document in the system is still part of the active information or knowledge collection by virtue of its database entry. When the document is no longer active and is ready to be archived, the database entry makes the transition a smooth one. In most cases, the time for long-term storage is set when the database entry is created.

Finally, when the document is destroyed, the database entry holds the record of that destruction, a critical requirement for any records management system. The key to the success of this system is the needs assessment that allows us to identify the organization's *who, how* and *what* and to use that knowledge to our client's advantage.

Chapter 7
Protecting for the Future

My father tells a story that has come to symbolize the complexity and necessity of archiving information. We're descended from pioneers and my father's family was one of the earliest to settle in Kansas. My great-grandfather was born in the 1870s, and not too long after he died in 1969, my father came across my grandmother burning letters from great-grandfather's house. Shocked and horrified, my father asked her what she was doing. "It's no one else's business," she calmly replied, tossing the last box of papers on the fire.

Years of stories, anecdotes, recipes and family news—all reduced to ashes in a few moments. What my grandmother saw as private information was a priceless collection of family history to me. Time alone would have turned what was once fresh cut and personal into a more benign reading of my heritage. At least, that's what I would have liked to tell my grandmother. I don't know if anyone could have ever convinced her of the value of those old letters and postcards. She simply could not see beyond her own beliefs and values.

If my grandmother had a vision for the future, I might have been able to read my great-great-grandmother's recollection of the Civil War. I might have seen discharge papers from that same war, and I might have read an account of a great-great-aunt's first dance. What a precious gift that would have been, both for our family and for our part of Kansas.

I share this story because I know that when it comes to corporate data, some companies share my grandmother's desire to protect what is seen as private. Rather than archive corporate memory—the good, the bad and the ugly—it's not unusual for organizations to restrict their recordkeeping to only what addresses legal obligations. What a waste, especially for those who want to be learning organizations. Learning from mistakes is as important as celebrating successes, and to preserve a complete history is a valuable gift for the present and the future. Fortunately, recordkeeping for legal requirements and to preserve the corporate memory can be addressed by the same, well-planned information system that we have explored in the previous chapters. My belief is that any record worth retaining, whether to meet retention obligations or for disaster recovery, is also worth using proper preservation methods.

Preservation: The Basics

R andy Silverman is the preservation librarian at the University of Utah's Marriott Library and can articulate better than anyone why we must address corporate archival issues. I asked Randy to help me articulate the necessity of preserving the corporate memory. A synthesis of our conversation follows.

SF: Why should we be concerned with preserving the corporate memory?

RS: There are multiple reasons. The first is because an institution is part of America. Even small companies play an important role in the community, state and nation. The institution's history is part of American history. We keep the records for legal and fiscal responsibility and beyond that, the long-term memory of the company helps us to understand achievements within the context of history. We see those in the events and speeches in the corporate collection.

Second, historical records are part of the company's heritage. Sometimes there is a fear that records retention for the corporate memory will mean there is a documentation of failures, too. But you have to have a sense of how you've grown and how you got there. You don't have to publish failures but you should keep it for the company's use. From these artifacts we can build retrospectives that help the company look back and perhaps learn new lessons.

In a nutshell, our responsibility to preserve records is guided by these factors:

1. fiscal/legal mandates
2. long-term merit for corporate history
3. place within culture (local, state and national)

SF: What has historical value?

RS: We have to keep in mind that the questions of the future will be different from what we've conceptualized in the present. Corporate records are used as part of research to describe culture—especially important in long-owned companies.

As an example, the Emporia State University's School of Library and Information Management is working with the National Park Service to establish an archival collection for the Rocky Mountain National Park. This project made us ask, "What of these records are interesting?" A percentage has to go to the regional office and personnel records go to Denver. Personnel records are closed and open to researchers long after the person is deceased.

Some records are mandated to be kept onsite, but there had not been much enforcement. One set of records that had dubious value were receipts for tour groups from the 1920s. Why should we keep these? After studying them, we realized that these receipts tell the story of how the park was developed, which roads were used, etc. Interestingly, the current condition of the park is traceable through those records. The point to this story is this: we don't always have the right questions to find out how these [old records] could be used. Sometimes we have to let the records tell us their story, and then we have new knowledge or a new perspective.

SF: When does value emerge?

RS: The time lapse varies but one thing is constant: scarcity is valued. Witness the value for original Coca-Cola memorabilia, and the associated prices collectors will pay for these items. Sometimes a company doesn't wait for the value to emerge. They have a long-term vision that says these items are worth keeping and investing in. In addition to Coca–Cola—which has a fascinating museum in Atlanta, Georgia—Walt Disney Company has had a long-term vision regarding preserving early works. Anyone who has been to the Disney facilities can appreciate the artifacts from the early years as well as more current documents.

We need to keep in mind that interest in the past often jumps a generation, so we should think of subsequent generations and preserve for the researcher of the future.

SF: What tools and expertise are needed to archive records?

RS: Obtain the training that will teach you about the tools, or—since training and higher education courses take time and money—consider hiring a consultant for a day or two. This option is much less expensive and that professional can help you develop a plan that is best for your organization.

If you do decide to "do it yourself," please understand that there are subtleties involved. For example, the order of how things were stored is part of the story. Carefully note the order of the artifacts and include that in the record—assuming that you have to split the collection to optimize individual artifact preservation.

SF: How do you decide what to keep?

RS: There are different levels of storage facilities, what we like to call "fat," "middle" and "lean." The "lean" level starts with the basics. A company needs a retention schedule and may want to consult with professionals to decide what to keep and for how long. The middle level includes storage materials, such as acid-free folders, tissue and other tools designed to maximize preservation. The top level, or "fat," includes climate-controlled storage, which can be expensive. [*Author's note:* In the Midwest, a one-and-one-half cubic foot climate-controlled storage space goes for about one hundred dollars a month.] Multiply those costs over the years, and preserved artifacts become very expensive. That calls for careful consideration of what you decide to keep.

Bottom line: Start at the lean and work up to the fat.

SF: How do I decide what to keep?

RS: Ask yourself, "What is the meat of the historic memory?" Then think about what would be secondary in importance. Some examples of items to keep:

- Staff photos—individual and group
- Building photos
- Giveaways
- Prototype products

Make sure you track down company archives; these can be in odd places, such as closets and working files in individuals' offices. It's possible to evolve a system from its current informal structure into a corporate library.

A word of caution about self-censorship: Be very careful about what you toss. A case in point is the current fad of scrapbooking. Although it is to be commended for its goal of preserving family memories, if applied to the corporate sector it becomes a dangerous process if you cut out background or important people. People in the future will not know what you've thrown away, and it could have had significance.

If your company has been around for a few years, ask yourself what it is about the early history that you find interesting. What do you wish you had more of? The answers will help you avoid creating a historical gap for future workers.

Finally, any organization wanting to start an archival collection should rely on outside help, such as consultants who can work with staff on this type of project. Start with expertise. Start smart. If you're at the middle level and in the market for archival boxes and folders, buy only high-quality products. Cheaper products will end up costing more money in the long run, once you realize that you have to replace everything with the high quality products you should have purchased in the first place.

The corporation needs to look for its own packrat to save the pieces that are needed to comprise a company archive. If the company is concerned about costs, there is always the option to donate the materials to an agency with an interest in preservation.

SF: Why not put everything online or burn it onto CD?

RS: The archival nightmares are numerous. What do you do with electronic data that no longer has a software of origin? What happens to electronic data if you convert it to the latest version of the software? It still loses coding, which means you lose part of the original document. Convert it enough times and you have meaningless data bits on your hard drive or server.

A better strategy is to—whenever possible—preserve artifacts in their original format. If the format is digital, find a backup format that will provide as much of the original content as is feasible. The message of Nicholson Baker's *Double Fold* (Random House, 2001) is underscored whenever one sees an historical display, such as front page newspapers from the World War II years. The actual artifact has more visual impact than a photocopy of a microfilm record. However, not every artifact is needed to produce an historical display. Storage costs and preservation realities mean that clients have to make choices about what to preserve, how and where—and the information professional can assist in developing the archival plan.

This is good advice from an expert in preservation— information we're obligated to share with our clients. Not every organization sees itself as an important part of the community, and yet, collectively, we are all creating history. It's part of our professional ethics to encourage companies and organizations who have not previously recognized their social responsibility to preserve their corporate memory to take Randy Silverman's advice and begin to take action.

Chapter 8

Information Flow

> "I took the road less traveled. And
> that has made all the difference."
> — Robert Frost

A
nd so we come full circle. We began this book talking
about the information profession and its philosophy of
people-centeredness as a means to success. Other professions may not define success as we do, for ours is one of the
few whose primary purpose is to contribute to the common
good. Within our framework of "people first," anytime we accurately diagnose an information need and provide an equally accurate solution, we have achieved success. Our success builds a
piece of Millay's loom that the world may be leached of its ills.

We established that people are at the center of what we do.
As information professionals, it is our responsibility to form professional relationships with our clients so that we may understand fully their information needs and processing preferences.
Only when we know our clients can we provide the value-
added, customized service that sets us apart from the "do-it-
yourself" approach.

The definitive answer to our clients' present and future information needs is the infrastructure built on the information
lifecycle. This system, best designed after a thorough assessment

of an organization's needs, addresses immediate and long-term needs and manages information at every point of its lifecycle. Organizations with this type of information infrastructure are in a better position to respond quickly to their environment because the infrastructure facilitates information flow for increased efficiency and productivity.

Information professionals can answer the occasional research request, and for many clients this is enough. For the organization that is heavily information-based, the implementation of a customized information infrastructure increases its ability to locate and retrieve the right information in the right format at the right time. This level of efficiency pays off in benefits many times its cost.

The success of this approach rests on the assumption of a commitment to the information profession and, by extension, to superb customer service. Our profession holds people as the most important component in any information-based relationship. As such, we seek to develop professional relationships that allow us to know our clients and how they use, create and reuse information. When we know our clients, we can provide customized service, including the design and implementation of a system appropriate to both current and future information needs.

If people are why we create customized information services then we also value those who create, analyze, diagnose and make recommendations. Recommendations must fit with the client's stated vision, mission and objectives, corporate culture and budget. At the same time, the professional looks at what will propel his or her client toward their stated goals. Decisions are weighted in favor of what practices and acquisitions will create the most efficient and lasting change possible.

Recommendations also have to fit the corporate learning style while making room for the individual's learning and information processing preferences. Clearly, this is impossible unless we carefully examine our clients' values, environment, goals and culture. Together the pieces tell us what the end product should look like, function as and accomplish.

A very wise man once said, "Professionals diagnose. It's what they do." Information professionals are no different. We draw on our profession's body of knowledge and our experience to analyze our client's situation and make recommendations. As with any prescription or professional advice, it may be necessary to reflect and reexamine and rediagnose until we have the perfect fit.

But I have already shared these points with you. The question before you now is, "What will you do with this information?" If you're an information professional, I hope you have found one or two ideas to use. I also encourage you to continually pursue professional growth. That may come through attending conferences and workshops; it is also accomplished by reading in a variety of subjects and having conversations with other professionals from a variety of disciplines.

If you are outside of the information profession but interested in increasing the value of your organization's information, I hope you will look for an information professional to help answer your questions. Please feel free to contact me if you need help in your search.

Whether you are an information professional or a client, I ask that wherever you practice, whomever you serve, be a weaver of knowledge.

Resources

Associations

Association of Independent Information Professionals (AIIP)
8550 United Plaza Blvd., Suite 1001
Baton Rouge, LA 70809
Phone: (225) 408-4400
Fax: (225) 922-4611

ARMA International
13725 W. 109th St., Suite 101
Lenexa, KS 66215
Phone: (913) 341-3808
Toll-free: (800) 422-2762 (U.S. and Canada)
Fax: (913) 341-3742

Consultants

Roger Greer, *Professor and Dean Emeritus*, Denver, Colorado
John Holland, *Database Developer*, Propaganda3, Kansas City,
  Missouri

Randy Silverman, *Preservation Librarian*, Marriott Library, University of Utah, Salt Lake City, UT

Instruments

The Myers-Briggs Type Indication (MBTI) is available through Consulting Psychologists Press, Inc. (CPP, Inc.):
CPP, Inc. and Davies-Black Publishing
3803 East Bayshore Road
P.O. Box 10096
Palo Alto, CA 94303
Tel: (650) 969-8901
Toll free: (800) 624-1765
Fax: (650) 969-8608

Publications

Cleveland, H. (1985). *The knowledge executive: Leadership in an information society.* New York: Truman Talley Books.

Gardner, H. (1983). *Frames of mind: The theory of multiple intelligences.* New York: Basic Books.

———. (1993). *Multiple intelligences: The theory in practice.* New York: Basic Books.

———. (1999). *Intelligence reframed.* New York: Basic Books.

Garvin, D. A. (1993). "Building a learning organization." *Harvard Business Review.*

Gephart, M. A., Marsick, V. J., Van Buren, M. E., and Spiro, M. S. (1996). "Learning organizations come alive." *Training and Development* 50 (12): 34.

Greengard, S. (October 1998) "Will your culture support KM? (knowledge management)(Knowledge Management: A Primer) *Workforce*, 77 (10): 93-94.

Grover, R. J., and Carabell, J. (Winter 1995). "Toward better information service: Diagnosing information needs." *Special Libraries* 86 (1).

Kuhlthau, C. C. (1993, 2003). *Seeking meaning: A process approach to library and information services.* Littleton, CO: Libraries Unlimited.

Lave, J., and Wenger, E. (1991). *Situated learning: Legitimate peripheral participation.* Cambridge: Cambridge University Press.

Lincoln, Y. S., and Guba, E. G. (1985, 1995). *Naturalistic inquiry.* Beverly Hills, CA: Sage Publications.

Stewart, T. A. (August 5, 1996). "The invisible key to success (Communities of Practice)." *Fortune* 134 (3) 173-75.

———. (2001). *The wealth of knowledge: Intellectual capital and the twenty-first century organization.* New York: Currency (Doubleday).

Van Maanen, J. (1988). *Tales of the field: On writing ethnography.* Chicago: University of Chicago Press.

Wenger, E. (February 1997). "Practice, learning, meaning, identity (learning concept 'communities of practice')." *Training* 34 (2): 38-39.

Wilson, P. (1977). *Public knowledge and private ignorance.* Westport, CT: Greenwood Press.

Zack, M. H. (Spring 1999). "Developing a knowledge strategy." *California Management Review* 41 (3).

Software Companies

Auto-Graphics, Inc.
3201 Temple Avenue
Pomona, CA 91768-3279

800-776-6939
909-595-7004
www4.auto-graphics.com/

Hummingbird, Ltd.
1 Sparks Ave.
Toronto, Ontario M2H 2W1, Canada
416-496-2200
877-359-4866
www.hummingbird.com

IBM
New Orchard Rd.
Armonk, NY 10504
914-499-1900
800-426-4968
www.ibm.com

Inmagic
200 Unicorn Park Drive, Fourth Floor
Woburn, MA 01801
781-938-4444
800-229-8398
www.inmagic.com

Percussion Software, Inc.
600 Unicorn Park Drive
Woburn, MA 01801
800-283-0800
781-438-9900
www.percussion.com

Sample Learning Styles Instrument

Date: _____

Name: _____

Job Title: _____

Job Duties: _____

Please check each statement that is true for you. Do not spend too much time on any question.

	TRUE
I like to see things completed according to plan.	
I like working with numbers.	
I often need time to myself to think things out.	
I like to "talk through" problems with other people.	
I like to listen to music while I read or work.	
I am often skeptical about new ideas.	
I am usually sensitive to others' feelings.	
I enjoy being in natural settings.	
I enjoy participating in discussions of all types.	
I enjoy writing.	
I understand information best if I can read it.	
I prefer to get information by listening.	
I am able to stay calm and objective during a crisis.	
I prefer to be physically active in my work.	
I express myself well in writing.	
I like to have a schedule to follow.	
I would rather be right than liked.	
I enjoy having quiet time by myself.	
I understand my abilities and limitations.	
I like things to be well-organized and structured.	
I like specific answers to specific questions.	

Sample Interview Questions

Question	Relevance
What are your (department, division) goals?	General
What are your (department, division) objectives?	General
What are the core business processes of your (department, division)?	General
How do you use information for monitoring progress?	Information use
How do you use information for making decisions?	Information use
How do you use information for managing projects?	Information use
How is information acquired: paper? people (face-to-face)? electronic?	Information intake
How is information stored: paper ? electronic ?	Information system
Where is the information stored: locally? in an organized repository?	Information system
How much information do you receive per month?	Information intake
What are the policy rules for promoting or discarding the information you receive from projects?	Information system
How many times a month do you receive requests for providing copies of information?	Information flow
Who requests information from you?	Information flow

Question	Relevance
Who makes these requests?	Information flow
How many times a month do you need/request information from projects directed by other coworkers?	Information flow
Who do you have the most contact with?	Information flow
Do you get all the information that you need?	Information need
Do you get the information in time?	Information need
Do you get the information in the format of your preference?	Information need
Which of the following formats do you prefer: paper ? electronic? both?	Information intake

Client Assessment: Who, How and What

Who

    Name   _____

    Role   _____

    Educational   ☐ High school/GED   ☐ BA/BS
    background   ☐ Master's   ☐ PhD/EdD

How

    Learning prefer-
    ences

        MBTI   _____
        Multiple intelli-
        gences (list)

What

    What will this
    information
    package be used
    for?
    What is the
    expected use?   _____
    Other notes:

                   _____

Index

About the Author

Susan G. Fowler earned a bachelor of arts in psychology from the University of Kansas in 1981 and a master's in library and information science (MLS) from Emporia State University in 1993. A lifelong learner, she continues her education in the library science field by taking and teaching postgraduate courses. The former include doctoral work in the area of information infrastructure and the learning organization; the latter include information entrepreneurship and database design. She is working on a legal information management certificate through a collaborative program sponsored by the University of Kansas School of Law and Emporia State University's School of Library and Information Management.

Ms. Fowler remains active in the information consulting business she founded immediately after earning her MLS. Her clients include organizations in the fields of law, healthcare and philanthropy. She is a member of the library and information science honor society Beta Phi Mu, American Library Association (ALA), Association of American Law Libraries (AALL), ARMA International and the Kansas Library Association (KLA).

She serves her local and state community through membership on a variety of committees. A native Kansan, Ms. Fowler resides with her husband and six cats on a portion of the family farm established in the 1850s.